3/5

30p.

50p

From Mum
19 90

Hope you can do some
of them climbs xx
xx

30p

Contents

Egg & Cheese Dishes

Mary Cadogan
Barbara Logan

Cheddar fries with spicy sauce

Preparation time: 15 minutes, plus chilling
Cooking time: 15 minutes

225 g/8 oz Cheddar cheese, cut into 1 cm/½ inch cubes

1 egg, beaten

100 g/4 oz brown breadcrumbs

oil for deep frying

salt

Sauce:

2 teaspoons oil

1 small onion, peeled and chopped

150 ml/¼ pint tomato ketchup

1 tablespoon Worcestershire sauce

2 tablespoons clear honey

2 tablespoons vinegar

1. Coat the cheese cubes in the beaten egg and breadcrumbs twice. Chill while making the sauce.
2. Heat the oil in a small saucepan and gently fry the onion for about 5 minutes until soft.
3. Add the remaining sauce ingredients. Simmer for 5 minutes until thickened.
4. Heat the oil to 180°C/350°F. Fry the cheese cubes, in 2 or 3 batches, for about 2 minutes until golden. Drain well on paper towels.
5. Sprinkle the fries with salt and serve with the spicy sauce.

Cheshire onion soup

Preparation time: 10 minutes
Cooking time: 20 minutes

175 g/6 oz Cheshire cheese

25 g/1 oz butter

1 large onion, peeled and thinly sliced

25 g/1 oz plain flour

300 ml/½ pint stock

450 ml/¾ pint milk

1 teaspoon made English mustard

salt

freshly ground black pepper

1 tablespoon chopped fresh parsley

1. Crumble the cheese between the fingers on to a plate.
2. Melt the butter in a large saucepan and gently fry the onion until soft and lightly browned.
3. Add the flour and cook, stirring, for 1 minute.
4. Gradually stir in the stock and milk. Bring to the boil, stirring until thickened and smooth.
5. Add the mustard, salt and pepper. Simmer for 10 minutes, stirring occasionally.
6. Stir in the cheese and parsley. Heat gently until the cheese has just melted, about 2 minutes. Serve immediately with crusty bread or toast.

Egg & tuna mousse

Serves 4 as a main course or 8 as a starter
Preparation time: 30 minutes
Cooking time: 10 minutes

1 x 275 g/10 oz can asparagus
  pieces

3 teaspoons gelatine

150 ml/¼ pint soured cream

3 tablespoons Mayonnaise
  (card 22)

2 tablespoons chopped onion

3 eggs, hard-boiled, shelled and
  chopped

1 teaspoon curry powder

1 x 200 g/7 oz. can tuna, drained
  and flaked

salt

freshly ground black pepper

1 egg white

To garnish:

cress

paprika

lettuce

stuffed olives

1. Drain the asparagus reserving
4 tablespoons of the liquid.
2. Sprinkle the gelatine over the reserved
liquid in a small heatproof bowl, then leave
until spongy. Stand the bowl in a pan of hot
water and heat gently until the gelatine has
dissolved, stirring occasionally.
3. In a basin mix together the soured
cream, asparagus pieces, mayonnaise,
onion, eggs, curry powder, tuna, salt and
pepper.
4. Stir in the dissolved gelatine.
5. Whisk the egg white until stiff and fold
into the mixture.
6. Pour into individual dishes or a fish
shaped mould and leave to set.
7. Garnish individual mousses with cress
and a sprinkling of paprika.
8. If using a mould turn the mousse out on
to a bed of lettuce and garnish with cress
and olives.
9. Serve as a starter with melba toast or as
a light meal with a salad and rolls.

Cheese & olive sablés

Makes about 20
Preparation time: 20 minutes, plus chilling
Cooking time: 15 minutes
Oven: 200°C, 400°F, Gas Mark 6

75 g/3 oz plain flour

pinch of salt

cayenne pepper

75 g/3 oz butter

25 g/1 oz Parmesan cheese, grated

50 g/2 oz Cheddar cheese, grated

about 20 stuffed olives

1. Place the flour, salt and a good pinch of cayenne pepper in a bowl. Add the butter, cut into small pieces, and rub into the flour with the fingertips.
2. Add the cheeses and draw the mixture together with the fingers to form a firm dough.
3. Turn out on to a floured surface and knead lightly until smooth.
4. Flatten a small piece of dough in the palm of the hand. Place an olive in the centre and bring the dough around the olive to enclose it.
5. Repeat with the remaining dough and olives. Chill for 30 minutes.
6. Place a little apart, on a baking sheet. Place in a preheated oven and bake for about 15 minutes until golden. Serve warm.

Cheese straws

Makes about 80
Preparation time: 15 minutes, plus chilling
Cooking time: 10-15 minutes
Oven: 200°C, 400°F, Gas Mark 6

175 g/6 oz plain flour

salt

2 teaspoons mustard powder

100 g/4 oz butter

50 g/2 oz Cheddar cheese, grated

25 g/1 oz Parmesan cheese, grated

1 egg, beaten

celery or poppy seeds

1. Place the flour, salt and mustard in a bowl. Add the butter, cut into small pieces, and rub in to the flour with the fingertips until the mixture resembles fine breadcrumbs.
2. Add the cheeses and mix well.
3. Add 2 tablespoons beaten egg and mix to form a firm dough.
4. Wrap the dough in cling film and chill for 10 minutes.
5. Roll out the dough and cut into lengths 7.5 cm/3 inches wide. Cut each length into 1 cm/½ inch strips.
6. Twist each strip and place on baking sheets. Brush with the remaining beaten egg and sprinkle with celery seeds or poppy seeds.
7. Place in a preheated oven and bake for 10-15 minutes until crisp and golden. Cool on a wire tray. Serve warm or cold.

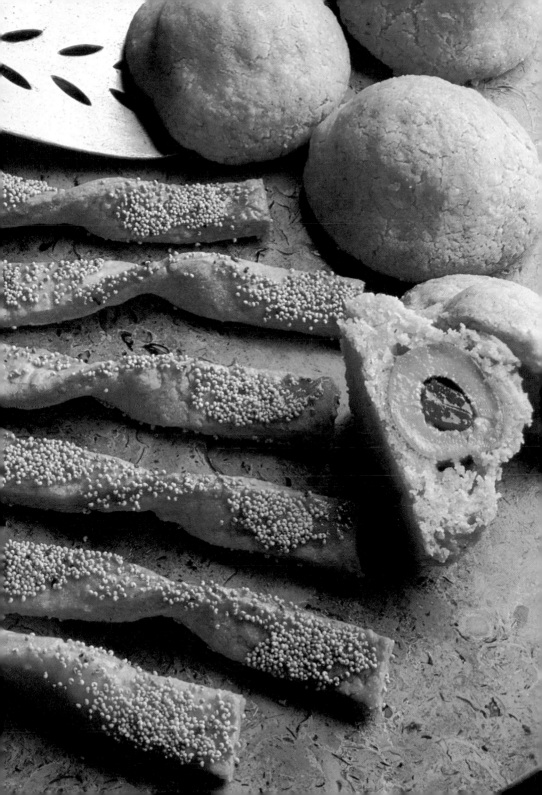

Roquefort & walnut toast

Preparation time: 5 minutes
Cooking time: 2 minutes

1 large slice bread

butter

50 g/2 oz Roquefort cheese,
  crumbled

2 teaspoons chopped walnuts

1 teaspoon chopped fresh
  parsley

1. Toast the bread and spread with butter.
2. Sprinkle over the Roquefort cheese and
walnuts. Place under a preheated grill until
the cheese has melted.
3. Sprinkle with chopped parsley and cut
into squares or fingers.

Blue cheese bites

Makes 40
Preparation time: 15 minutes

25 g/1 oz unsalted butter,
  softened

75 g/3 oz full fat soft (cream)
  cheese

50 g/2 oz blue cheese, e.g. Stilton
  or Danish blue, grated

freshly ground black pepper

2 tablespoons chopped fresh
  parsley, paprika or 25 g/1 oz
  walnuts, finely chopped

1. Place the butter and full fat soft cheese in
a bowl. Beat with a wooden spoon until well
mixed.
2. Add the blue cheese and pepper. Beat
until well mixed. If the mixture is too soft to
handle, chill for 30 minutes.
3. Form the mixture into tiny balls. Roll in
the chopped parsley, paprika or walnuts.
4. Serve on cocktail sticks.

Garlic & herb dip

Preparation time: 5 minutes

225 g/8 oz medium fat soft
  (curd) cheese

3 tablespoons milk

1 tablespoon chopped fresh
  herbs, e.g. parsley, oregano,
  mint

1 garlic clove, peeled and
  crushed

salt

freshly ground black pepper

1. Place the cheese in a bowl. Beat in the
milk gradually until smooth.
2. Add the herbs, garlic, salt and pepper.
Mix well.
3. Transfer to a serving dish and serve with
crisp sticks of raw vegetables, cauliflower
florets or savoury crackers.

Onion & cream quiche

Preparation time: 25-30 minutes
Cooking time: 35-40 minutes
Oven: 200°C, 400°F, Gas Mark 6;
      190°C, 375°F, Gas Mark 5

175 g/6 oz plain flour

pinch of salt

75 g/3 oz fat

40 g/1½ oz Cheddar cheese, grated

pinch of dry mustard

cold water

Filling:

50 g/2 oz butter

450 g/1 lb onions, peeled and sliced

3 eggs

200 ml/⅓ pint single cream

salt

freshly ground black pepper

¼ teaspoon dried dill weed

1. Sift the flour and salt into a mixing bowl. Cut the fat into pieces and rub into the flour until the mixture resembles fine breadcrumbs.
2. Add the cheese, mustard and enough cold water to mix to a firm dough. Knead lightly then roll out and use to line a 20 cm/8 inch flan ring placed on a baking sheet.
3. Line with a piece of foil and cook in a preheated oven for 10 minutes.
4. Remove the foil and set the pastry case on one side. Reduce the oven temperature.
5. Melt the butter in a saucepan, add the onion and fry until soft. Put into the pastry case.
6. Beat together the eggs, cream, salt, pepper and dill weed. Pour into the pastry case.
7. Cook in the preheated oven for 25-30 minutes.
8. Serve as a main meal with courgettes and duchesse potatoes.

Variation:
Leek and ham quiche: In place of the onions use sliced leeks and add 100 g/4 oz chopped ham to the filling.

Spinach & ricotta pie

Preparation time: 30 minutes, plus chilling
Cooking time: about 1¼ hours
Oven: 200°C, 400°F, Gas Mark 6

350 g/12 oz plain flour

1 teaspoon salt

75 g/3 oz butter or margarine

75 g/3 oz lard

4 tablespoons cold water

milk or beaten egg, to glaze

Filling:

450 g/1 lb spinach, washed

25 g/1 oz butter

100 g/4 oz mushrooms, finely
   chopped

4 eggs, lightly beaten

1 teaspoon dried oregano

salt

freshly ground black pepper

450 g/1 lb Ricotta cheese

25 g/1 oz plain flour

120 ml/4 fl oz milk

If you are unable to buy Ricotta cheese for the filling, sieved cottage cheese or medium fat soft (curd) cheese also work well.

1. Place the flour and salt in a mixing bowl. Add the butter and lard, cut into small pieces, and rub into the flour with the fingertips until the mixture resembles fine breadcrumbs.
2. Add the water and mix to form a firm dough. Wrap in cling film and chill.
3. To make the filling, cook the spinach with no extra water in a covered saucepan for about 10 minutes until tender. Drain well, pressing out as much water as possible, and chop finely.
4. Melt the butter in a pan and fry the mushrooms for about 2 minutes.
5. Remove the mushrooms from the heat and stir in half the beaten eggs, the spinach, oregano, salt and pepper.
6. Mix the cheese, flour, remaining eggs and milk together. Add salt and pepper to taste.
7. Roll out just over half of the pastry and use to line a 25 cm/10 inch flan tin. Place spoonsful of the Ricotta cheese filling around the outside 5 cm/2 inches of the base. Fill the centre with the spinach filling.
8. Roll out the remaining pastry, dampen the edges and cover the pie.
9. Trim off the excess pastry with a knife, roll out and cut into strips. Brush the top of the pie with a little milk or beaten egg and arrange a lattice of pastry strips across the top. Brush again with milk or egg.
10. Place in a preheated oven and bake for about 1 hour until the pastry is golden brown. Serve warm or cold.

Mozzarella turnovers

Preparation time: 40 minutes, plus resting
Cooking time: about 15 minutes

225 g/8 oz plain flour

1 teaspoon salt

1 teaspoon paprika

50 g/2 oz lard

1 tablespoon oil

120 ml/4 fl oz water

Filling:

25 g/1 oz butter

1 medium onion, peeled and chopped

175 g/6 oz Italian Mozzarella cheese, cubed

1 egg, beaten

½ teaspoon salt

1 tablespoon chopped fresh parsley

1 teaspoon chopped fresh mixed herbs

oil for deep frying

1. Place the flour, salt and paprika in a mixing bowl, mix with a fork.
2. Heat the lard, oil and water in a pan until the lard has just melted. Remove from the heat and stir into the flour to form a soft dough.
3. Turn out on to a lightly floured surface and knead until smooth. Wrap in cling film and leave to rest for 30 minutes.
4. To make the filling, melt the butter in a pan and fry the onion for about 5 minutes until soft and lightly browned.
5. Add the cheese, egg, salt and herbs. Heat gently, for about 2 minutes, stirring until smooth. Cool slightly.
6. Roll out the pastry and cut into 8 x 13 cm/5 inch squares. Divide the filling between the squares. Dampen the edges of the pastry and fold over diagonally. Pinch the edges to seal.
7. Heat the oil to 180°C, 350°F, or until a cube of bread browns in 30 seconds. Fry the turnovers, a few at a time, for about 3 minutes until golden. Drain on paper towels.

Prawn & egg curry

Preparation time: 25 minutes
Cooking time: 35-40 minutes

3 tablespoons oil

100 g/4 oz onions, peeled and
  sliced

1 large cooking apple, peeled,
  cored and chopped

2-3 tablespoons curry powder

1 tablespoon plain flour

1 tablespoon mango chutney

2 teaspoons tomato purée

50 g/2 oz sultanas

1 tablespoon demerara sugar

1 x 300 g/11 oz can pineapple
  cubes

about 450 ml/¾ pint light stock
  or water

175 ml/6 fl oz soured cream

175-225 g/6-8 oz peeled prawns

9 eggs, hard-boiled and shelled

225 g/8 oz long-grain rice

To serve:

desiccated coconut

mango chutney

sliced banana in lemon juice

peanuts

poppadoms

1. Heat the oil in a saucepan, add the onion and fry for 5-6 minutes. Add the apple and fry for a further 2-3 minutes.

2. Stir in the curry powder, flour, chutney, tomato purée, sultanas and sugar, and cook for 3-4 minutes.

3. Drain the juice from the can of pineapple and make up to 600 ml/1 pint with the stock or water. Stir the liquid into the saucepan, bring to the boil, cover and simmer for 20-25 minutes.

4. Add the pineapple, reserving a few pieces, the soured cream, prawns and 8 whole eggs. Heat for a further 5 minutes. Slice the remaining egg.

5. Cook the rice in boiling salted water for 12-15 minutes until just cooked, drain and put into a serving dish.

6. Arrange the whole eggs on top and pour the sauce over. Garnish with the sliced egg and remaining pineapple.

7. Serve with individual dishes of coconut, chutney, banana and peanuts and with poppadoms.

Eggs fruits de mer

Preparation time: 10 minutes
Cooking time: 20 minutes

50 g/2 oz butter

40 g/1½ oz plain flour

450 ml/¾ pint milk

3 tablespoons single cream

3 tablespoons white wine

2 egg yolks

salt

freshly ground black pepper

8 eggs, hard-boiled, shelled and halved

1 x 75 g/3 oz can smoked oysters

1 x 100 g/4 oz jar baby clams, drained

1 x 150 g/5 oz jar mussels, drained

2 tablespoons browned breadcrumbs

fleurons of puff pastry, to garnish

1. Melt the butter in a saucepan, add the flour and cook for 1-2 minutes.
2. Gradually stir in the milk, and stirring constantly, simmer for 2-3 minutes.
3. Stir in the cream, wine, egg yolks, salt and pepper. Keep the sauce hot but do not allow to boil.
4. Arrange the egg halves in a shallow flameproof dish and add the oysters, clams and mussels.
5. Pour over the sauce, sprinkle with breadcrumbs and place under a preheated hot grill for 2-3 minutes.
6. Garnish with the fleurons, or insert triangles of toast round the edge. Serve with a green salad.

Variation: In place of oysters, clams and mussels use: 1 x 200 g/7 oz can shrimps, drained and 1 x 150 g/5 oz jar cockles, drained.

Eggs with watercress

Serves 4 as a main course or 8 as a starter

2 bunches of watercress

5 tablespoons Mayonnaise (card 22)

salt

freshly ground black pepper

finely grated rind and juice of ½ lemon

8 eggs

paprika

3 tomatoes, sliced

50 g/2 oz onions, peeled and thinly sliced

2 tablespoons French dressing

chopped fresh parsley, to garnish

1. Remove the tough stalks from the watercress, wash well and put into a saucepan. Cover with cold water, bring to the boil, cover and simmer for 10 minutes.
2. Drain well, and chop finely.
3. Mix together the watercress, 3 tablespoons of the mayonnaise, salt, pepper, lemon rind and juice, and spread the mixture over the bottom of a flat plate.
4. Boil the eggs for 5 minutes, shell and arrange them on the watercress.
5. Spoon the remaining mayonnaise over the top of the eggs and sprinkle with paprika.
6. Arrange the sliced tomatoes and onion alternately round the edge of the plate, spoon over the French dressing and sprinkle with parsley. Serve as a light meal, or with melba toast as a starter. This is also good for a buffet.

Cheese & smoked mackerel gougère

Preparation time: 20 minutes
Cooking time: 40 minutes
Oven: 200°C, 400°F, Gas Mark 6

150 ml/¼ pint water
50 g/2 oz butter
65 g/2½ oz plain flour
2 eggs, beaten
pinch of salt
75 g/3 oz Cheddar cheese, grated

Filling:

175 g/6 oz smoked mackerel, skinned and flaked
450 g/1 lb tomatoes, skinned and chopped
1 tablespoon chopped fresh parsley
salt
freshly ground black pepper
25 g/1 oz Cheddar cheese, grated

1. Place the water and butter in a saucepan. Heat until the butter has melted, then bring to the boil.

2. Remove from heat and quickly add the flour, all at once. Beat until the mixture leaves the sides of the pan.

3. Return to the heat and cook for 1 minute. Remove pan from the heat.

4. Cool slightly, then beat in the egg, a little at a time. Stir in the salt and 75 g/3 oz cheese.

5. To make the filling, mix together the mackerel, tomatoes, parsley, salt and pepper.

6. Spread the cheese choux pastry around the edge of a buttered 1.75 litre/3 pint ovenproof dish.

7. Pour the filling in the centre and sprinkle with the cheese.

8. Place in a preheated oven and bake for 35 minutes until risen and golden brown.

Crab & cheese mousse

Preparation time: 20 minutes, plus chilling

1 x 150 g/5 oz can crab meat, drained, reserving juice
100 g/4 oz Cheddar cheese, finely grated
150 ml/¼ pint double cream
2 tablespoons tomato ketchup
1 tablespoon lemon juice
salt
pinch of cayenne pepper
15 g/½ oz gelatine
2 egg whites

Garnish:

thin slices of cucumber
sprigs of watercress

1. Place the drained crab meat in a large bowl. Flake with a fork.

2. Add the cheese, cream, ketchup, lemon juice, salt and cayenne pepper. Mix well.

3. Place the reserved juice from the can of crab in a small bowl or cup. Sprinkle with the gelatine. Place in a saucepan of hot water and stir until dissolved.

4. Stir the dissolved gelatine thoroughly into the crab mixture.

5. Whisk the egg whites until stiff. Fold into the crab mixture with a metal spoon, cutting through the mixture until all the egg white is evenly incorporated.

6. Pour the mixture into a wetted 20 cm/ 8 inch ring mould. Chill for about 2 hours until set.

7. Turn the mould out on to a serving plate. Garnish with the cucumber and watercress.

Steak with Stilton

Preparation time: 10 minutes, plus chilling
Cooking time: 10 minutes

75 g/3 oz Stilton cheese, at room temperature

50 g/2 oz butter, softened

1 tablespoon lemon juice

4 sirloin or rump steaks

oil

freshly ground black pepper

sprigs of watercress, to garnish

1. Crumble the Stilton into a small bowl. Add the butter and lemon juice, and beat together until smooth and well mixed.
2. Place the mixture in a piece of foil or greaseproof paper large enough to completely enclose it. Form into a roll about 2.5 cm/1 inch wide. Wrap and chill for about 1 hour.
3. Rub the steaks with a little oil and sprinkle with pepper.
4. Place the steaks under a preheated hot grill and cook for 2-5 minutes each side, depending on your taste.
5. Serve the steaks on hot plates, topped with overlapping slices of Stilton butter. Garnish with the watercress.

Cheese pilaff

Preparation time: 15 minutes
Cooking time: about 50 minutes
Oven: 180°C, 350°F, Gas Mark 4

50 g/2 oz butter

1 large onion, peeled and sliced

1 red pepper, cored, seeded and sliced

225 g/8 oz courgettes, sliced

225 g/8 oz brown rice, washed and drained

½ teaspoon ground turmeric

½ teaspoon cayenne

1-2 teaspoons salt

freshly ground black pepper

750 ml/1¼ pints hot stock

175 g/6 oz Cheddar cheese, grated

1. Melt the butter in a flameproof casserole and fry the onion for about 5 minutes.
2. Add the red pepper, courgettes, rice, turmeric, cayenne, salt and pepper. Fry for 2 minutes, stirring.
3. Add the hot stock and cover with a well-fitting lid. Place in a preheated oven and cook for 45 minutes until the rice is tender and the stock absorbed.
4. Stir in the cheese until melted and serve hot.

Baked wheatmeal pancakes

Preparation time: 20 minutes
Cooking time: 35 minutes
Oven: 190°C, 375°F, Gas Mark 5

50 g/2 oz wheatmeal flour
salt
50 g/2 oz plain flour
1 egg
300 ml/½ pint milk
oil for shallow frying

Filling:

25 g/1 oz butter
25 g/1 oz plain flour
150 ml/¼ pint milk
salt
freshly ground black pepper
½ teaspoon celery seeds
1 tablespoon chopped fresh parsley
100 g/4 oz cooked ham, cut into small cubes
1 egg, beaten
150 g/5 oz Cheddar cheese, grated

1. Place the wheatmeal flour and salt in a bowl. Sift in the plain flour. Make a well in the centre and add the egg.

2. Beat in the milk gradually, drawing in the flour from the sides, until the batter is smooth and glossy.

3. Heat a little oil in an 18 cm/7 inch frying pan. Pour off the excess.

4. Pour in enough batter to thinly coat the base of the pan. Cook until the underside is golden brown, then turn over with a palette knife to complete cooking.

5. Slide the pancake on to a heated plate and keep warm while making the remaining pancakes. This amount of batter will make 8 pancakes.

6. Melt the butter in a saucepan. Stir in the flour and cook for 1 minute.

7. Remove from the heat and gradually stir in the milk. Add the salt, pepper and celery seeds. Bring to the boil and simmer for 2 minutes, stirring occasionally, until thickened and smooth.

8. Remove from the heat and add the parsley, ham, beaten egg and 100 g/4 oz of the cheese. Stir well.

9. Spread a little filling across the centre of each pancake and roll up. Arrange in a buttered shallow ovenproof dish.

10. Sprinkle with the remaining cheese. Place in a preheated oven and bake for 20 minutes until the cheese topping is golden brown.

Two-cheese pizza

Preparation time: 25 minutes, plus rising
Cooking time: 1 hour
Oven: 200°C, 400°F, Gas Mark 6

150 ml/¼ pint warm water

1 teaspoon sugar

1 teaspoon dried yeast

225 g/8 oz wheatmeal flour

1 teaspoon salt

15 g/½ oz butter

Topping:

1 tablespoon olive oil

1 garlic clove, peeled and
   crushed

1 onion, peeled and sliced

1 x 400 g/14 oz can tomatoes

2 tablespoons tomato purée

1 teaspoon chopped fresh
   oregano or ½ teaspoon dried
   oregano

1 teaspoon brown sugar

salt

freshly ground black pepper

100 g/4 oz Mozzarella cheese,
   sliced

100 g/4 oz Danish blue or Stilton
   cheese, sliced

1 tablespoon capers, drained

4 anchovies, drained

10 stuffed olives

1. Measure the water into a jug. Add the sugar and yeast, and leave for 10 minutes until frothy.

2. Place the flour and salt in a bowl. Rub in the butter. Add the yeast liquid all at once and mix to a soft dough.

3. On a floured surface, knead the dough for 5 minutes until smooth and pliable. Place the dough in an oiled polythene bag and leave for about 30 minutes to rise.

4. Meanwhile, to make the topping, heat the oil in a saucepan and gently fry the garlic and onion for about 10 minutes until softened.

5. Add the tomatoes, tomato purée, oregano, sugar, salt and pepper. Bring to the boil and simmer gently for about 20 minutes until thickened. Leave to cool.

6. Roll out the dough to a 30 cm/12 inch round. Place on an oiled baking sheet.

7. Spread the tomato sauce over the dough to within 1 cm/½ inch of the edge.

8. Arrange alternate slices of Mozzarella and blue cheese in triangles around the top of the pizza.

9. Chop the capers and anchovies together. Sprinkle over the pizza. Top with the stuffed olives.

10. Place in a preheated oven and bake for 25-30 minutes until the dough is golden brown and the cheeses have melted.

Cheese soufflé with poached eggs

Preparation time: 20 minutes
Cooking time: 45 minutes
Oven: 200°C, 400°F, Gas Mark 6

6 eggs

50 g/2 oz butter

50 g/2 oz plain flour

300 ml/½ pint milk

salt

freshly ground black pepper

100 g/4 oz Leicester cheese,
  grated

1. Fill a large pan with 2.5 cm/1 inch water. Heat until just simmering.
2. Carefully slide in 4 of the eggs and poach until the whites have just set. Remove from the pan with a slotted spoon and keep warm in a bowl of warm water.
3. Melt the butter in a saucepan. Stir in the flour and cook for 1 minute.
4. Remove from the heat and gradually stir in the milk. Bring to the boil and simmer for 2 minutes, stirring occasionally, until thickened and smooth.
5. Separate the remaining 2 eggs. Remove the sauce from the heat and beat in the salt, pepper, egg yolks and cheese.
6. Whisk the egg whites until stiff. Fold into the cheese mixture with a metal spoon, cutting through the mixture until all the egg white is evenly incorporated.
7. Pour half the mixture into a buttered 1.5 litre/2½ pint soufflé dish. Drain the poached eggs and blot with paper towels.
8. Place the eggs in the soufflé dish and cover with the remaining mixture.
9. Put the dish on a baking sheet. Place in a preheated oven and bake for 30-35 minutes until light and fluffy. Serve immediately.

Swiss fondue

1 garlic clove, peeled

450 ml/¾ pint dry white wine

1 teaspoon lemon juice

350 g/12 oz Gruyère cheese, finely grated

350 g/12 oz Emmenthal cheese, finely grated

1 tablespoon cornflour

3 tablespoons Kirsch

salt

freshly ground black pepper

French bread, cut into chunks

1. Cut the garlic clove in half and rub the cut surfaces around a fondue pot or heavy saucepan. Add the wine and lemon juice to the pot and heat gently until just bubbling.

2. Add a little cheese and stir until just melted. Add the remaining cheese, a little at a time, stirring with each addition, until melted.

3. Blend the cornflour with the Kirsch. Stir into the pan and cook over a low heat for about 3 minutes until thickened.

4. Add salt and pepper to taste. Serve immediately. Spear French bread on to long fondue forks and dip into the fondue.

Mayonnaise

Makes about 300 ml/½ pint
Preparation time: 15-20 minutes

2 egg yolks

½ teaspoon salt

freshly ground black pepper

¼ teaspoon dry mustard

¼ teaspoon caster sugar
  (optional)

1 tablespoon wine vinegar

1 tablespoon lemon juice

300 ml/½ pint olive oil

1. Put the yolks, salt, pepper, mustard, sugar, vinegar and lemon juice into a basin and whisk together well.
2. Gradually beat in the oil, drop by drop. As the mixture thickens the oil can be added in a thin stream until completely blended.
3. Taste and adjust the seasoning.

Bearnaise sauce

Makes about 150 ml/¼ pint
Preparation time: 5 minutes
Cooking time: 10-15 minutes

25 g/1 oz chopped shallot

6 peppercorns

1 tablespoon tarragon vinegar

2 egg yolks

25 g/1 oz softened butter

salt

juice of ½ lemon

2 teaspoons chopped fresh
  tarragon

1 teaspoon chopped fresh
  chervil

1. Put the shallot, peppercorns and vinegar into a saucepan, boil to reduce to half quantity, strain into a heatproof basin and allow to cool.
2. Add the egg yolks and whisk over a saucepan of hot water over a low heat, until pale in colour and thick enough to coat the back of a wooden spoon.
3. Gradually whisk in the butter then remove the basin from the heat.
4. Stir in the salt, lemon juice, tarragon and chervil.
5. Serve with steaks and grilled meat.

Hollandaise sauce

Makes about 300 ml/½ pint
Preparation time: 5 minutes
Cooking time: 10-15 minutes

2 tablespoons wine vinegar

2 tablespoons water

3 egg yolks

100 g/4 oz softened butter, cut
  into pieces

2 tablespoons lemon juice

salt

freshly ground black pepper

This sauce can be kept warm by putting the basin over a saucepan of hot water, but do not use any heat.

1. Boil the vinegar in a saucepan until reduced to half quantity, add the water and pour into a heatproof basin.
2. Add the egg yolks, put the basin over a saucepan of hot water over a low heat, and whisk continuously until thick enough to coat the back of a wooden spoon.
3. Gradually whisk in the butter, and then the lemon juice, salt and pepper.
4. Serve the sauce warm with fish, chicken, asparagus or broccoli.

Cheese, celery & grape salad

Preparation time: 10 minutes

4 sticks celery, finely chopped

100 g/4 oz black grapes, halved
  and seeded

225 g/8 oz Cheshire cheese,
  crumbled

Dressing:

100 g/4 oz apple purée

3 tablespoons mayonnaise

salt

freshly ground black pepper

This salad can be made several hours in advance. Cover with cling film and chill until needed.

1. Mix the celery, grapes and cheese in a bowl.
2. Mix together the dressing ingredients until smooth. Add to the salad and stir well.
3. Transfer the salad to a serving dish. Garnish with celery leaves, if liked.

Greek salad

Preparation time: 15 minutes

½ Iceberg lettuce, shredded

1 Spanish onion, peeled and
  thinly sliced

½ cucumber, thinly sliced

2 tablespoons chopped fresh
  parsley

1 green pepper, cored, seeded
  and cut into thin strips

3 small tomatoes, cut into small
  wedges

175 g/6 oz Feta cheese, cut into
  small cubes

10 black olives

Dressing:

5 tablespoons olive oil

2 tablespoons wine vinegar

1 tablespoon capers, finely
  chopped

salt

freshly ground black pepper

1. Place the lettuce, onion, cucumber, parsley and green pepper in a salad bowl. Add the tomato wedges to the bowl; mix well.
2. Place all the dressing ingredients in a screw-topped jar. Shake well to mix.
3. Toss the salad in the dressing just before serving. Sprinkle over the cheese and olives.

Green salad with blue cheese dressing

Preparation time: 10 minutes

1 crisp lettuce

Selection of salad leaves, e.g.
    endive, corn salad, spinach

½ cucumber, cut into
    matchstick pieces

1 punnet mustard and cress,
    washed

1 small green pepper, cored,
    seeded and cut into thin strips

1 avocado, halved, skinned and
    thinly sliced

25 g/1 oz walnuts, chopped

Dressing:

100 g/4 oz Stilton or Danish blue
    cheese, grated

150 ml/¼ pint soured cream

1 teaspoon clear honey

salt

freshly ground black pepper

1. Wash the lettuce and salad leaves, and pat dry with paper towels.
2. Shred the leaves with the fingers into a salad bowl. Sprinkle over the cucumber, mustard and cress and green pepper.
3. Arrange the avocado slices in the salad bowl and sprinkle with the walnuts.
4. Mix together the dressing ingredients in a bowl. Pour over the salad and toss just before serving, or serve separately if preferred.

Herbed tomato & Mozzarella salad

Preparation time: 5 minutes

450 g/1 lb tomatoes, thinly sliced

1 Italian Mozzarella (about
    175 g/6 oz), thinly sliced

Dressing:

1 garlic clove, peeled and
    crushed

3 tablespoons olive oil

1 tablespoon lemon juice

salt

freshly ground black pepper

1 tablespoon chopped fresh
    mixed herbs, e.g. oregano, basil,
    parsley, thyme

1. Arrange the tomato slices and cheese in alternate rows on a flat serving plate.
2. Place all the dressing ingredients in a screw-topped jar. Shake well to mix.
3. Pour the dressing over the salad just before serving.

Blue cheese salad

Preparation time: 15 minutes

4 tablespoons oil

1 garlic clove, peeled and crushed

3 thick slices bread, cut into cubes

1 crisp lettuce, shredded

bunch of watercress, trimmed and washed

1 chicory, sliced

225 g/8 oz blue cheese, e.g. Danish blue, Stilton or Roquefort, crumbled or cubed

Dressing:

150 ml/¼ pint plain unsweetened yogurt

2 teaspoons light Dijon mustard

1 teaspoon clear honey

salt

freshly ground black pepper

1. Heat the oil in a frying pan and gently fry the garlic for 1 minute.
2. Add the bread cubes and fry until evenly browned, turning occasionally. Drain the bread cubes on paper towels.
3. Place the lettuce, watercress and chicory in a salad bowl. Toss lightly.
4. Sprinkle the cheese into the bowl with the bread cubes.
5. Mix together the dressing ingredients in a small bowl. Pour over the salad and toss just before serving, or serve separately.

Slimmers' salad

Serves 2 as a main meal
Preparation time: 15 minutes

2 rashers streaky bacon, rinds removed

1 small bunch radishes, trimmed and thinly sliced

1 green pepper, cored, seeded and chopped

½ cucumber, chopped

225 g/8 oz cottage cheese

1 small bunch chives

½ teaspoon finely grated lemon rind

2 tablespoons lemon juice

salt

freshly ground black pepper

1. Grill the bacon until crisp. Drain well on paper towels. Crumble into small pieces.
2. Place the radishes in a bowl with the pepper, cucumber and cheese. Snip the chives into the bowl. Add the lemon rind and juice, salt and pepper; mix well.
3. Transfer the salad to a serving dish and sprinkle with the bacon pieces.

Eggs provençal

Preparation time: 10-15 minutes
Cooking time: 20-25 minutes
Oven: 190°C, 375°F, Gas Mark 5

4 tablespoons oil

225 g/8 oz onions, peeled and sliced

2 garlic cloves, peeled and crushed

225 g/8 oz courgettes, sliced

½ teaspoon mixed dried herbs

2 tablespoons chopped fresh parsley

1 x 400 g/14 oz can tomatoes

salt

freshly ground black pepper

4 eggs

1. Heat the oil in a pan, add the onions and garlic and fry for 3-4 minutes. Add the courgettes and fry for a further 3-4 minutes.
2. Stir in the herbs, parsley, salt, pepper and tomatoes. Put the mixture into an ovenproof dish.
3. Make 4 hollows and break an egg into each. Cook in a preheated oven for 10-15 minutes or until the eggs are set.

Hidden eggs

Preparation time: 10 minutes
Cooking time: 10-15 minutes
Oven: 180°C, 350°F, Gas Mark 4

65 g/2½ oz butter

1 tablespoon finely chopped onion

100 g/4 oz mushrooms, chopped

1 tablespoon chopped fresh parsley

salt

freshly ground black pepper

½ teaspoon dried basil

4 large tomatoes

4 eggs

4 slices buttered toast

watercress, to garnish

1. Use 15 g/½ oz of the butter to grease a shallow, medium ovenproof dish.
2. Melt 25 g/1 oz of the butter in a frying pan, add the onion and mushrooms and fry until soft. Stir in the parsley, salt, pepper and basil.
3. Cut a slice from the top of each tomato, carefully scoop out the pulp and put the tomato shells into the prepared dish.
4. Put some mushroom mixture into each tomato and break an egg on top.
5. Sprinkle with salt and pepper and dot each with the remaining butter. Replace the slice of tomato and cook in a preheated oven for 8-10 minutes or until the eggs are set.
6. Cut rounds of toast slightly larger than the tomatoes and place one under each tomato.
7. Garnish with watercress and serve as a starter.

Chicory & ham bake

Preparation time: 25 minutes
Cooking time: 45 minutes
Oven: 180°C, 350°F, Gas Mark 4

25 g/1 oz butter

4 heads chicory, trimmed

4 tablespoons water

1 tablespoon lemon juice

salt

freshly ground black pepper

4 slices cooked ham

250 ml/8 fl oz milk

75 g/3 oz Gruyère or Cheddar
cheese, grated

2 eggs, lightly beaten

1. Heat the butter in a large saucepan and coat the chicory in butter. Add the water, lemon juice, salt and pepper.

2. Cover and cook gently for about 15 minutes.

3. Remove the chicory from the pan with a slotted spoon. Wrap a slice of ham round each one. Place in a buttered ovenproof dish.

4. Add the milk, cheese, salt and pepper to the eggs. Pour over the chicory.

5. Place in a preheated oven and bake, uncovered, for 30 minutes until the sauce is set and the top is golden brown.

Variations:

Use celery instead of chicory.
Trim 1 head of celery to even lengths. Cook as for the chicory, reducing the cooking time to 10 minutes. Divide the celery sticks between slices of ham and roll up.
Use garlic sausage instead of cooked ham. You will need 8 slices of garlic sausage, 2 for each chicory head.

Aubergine & cheese pie

Preparation time: 25 minutes
Cooking time: 45 minutes
Oven: 200°C, 400°F, Gas Mark 6

2 medium aubergines

1 egg, beaten

75 g/3 oz wholewheat
  breadcrumbs

6 tablespoons olive oil

1 x 400 g/14 oz can tomatoes

1/2 teaspoon dried oregano

1 garlic clove, peeled and
  crushed

1 teaspoon sugar

salt

freshly ground black pepper

175 g/6 oz Mozzarella cheese,
  thinly sliced

4 tablespoons grated Parmesan
  cheese

1. Cut the aubergines into 5 mm/1/4 inch thick slices. Brush the slices with the beaten egg, then coat in the breadcrumbs.
2. Heat half the olive oil in a large pan and fry half the aubergine slices for about 5 minutes, turning once, until golden brown. Remove from the pan. Heat the remaining oil and fry the remaining aubergine slices.
3. Place the tomatoes, oregano, garlic, sugar, salt and pepper in a liquidizer. Blend until smooth. Alternatively, press through a sieve.
4. Place the aubergines in a 2.25 litre/4 pint ovenproof dish. Sprinkle with salt and pepper. Cover with the Mozzarella cheese, then pour over the tomato sauce.
5. Sprinkle with the Parmesan cheese. Place in a preheated oven and cook, uncovered, for 35 minutes.

Cheese & tomato pudding

Preparation time: 20 minutes, plus standing
Cooking time: 30-40 minutes
Oven: 200°C, 400°F, Gas Mark 6

4 large slices bread, crusts
  removed

3 eggs, separated

300 ml/1/2 pint milk

1/2 teaspoon salt

freshly ground black pepper

175 g/6 oz Double Gloucester
  cheese, grated

4 tomatoes, skinned, seeded and
  chopped

2 teaspoons Worcestershire
  sauce

1. Break up the bread and place in a bowl with the egg yolks. Place the egg whites in a separate bowl.
2. Heat the milk to just below boiling. Pour over the bread and mix with a fork. Leave for 20 minutes.
3. Add salt, pepper and the cheese to the bread. Mix well.
4. Whisk the egg whites until stiff. Fold into the cheese mixture, cutting through with a metal spoon, until all the egg white is incorporated.
5. Place the tomatoes in a buttered 1.75 litre/3 pint ovenproof pie dish. Sprinkle with the Worcestershire sauce and cover with the cheese mixture.
6. Place in a preheated oven and bake for 30-40 minutes until risen and golden brown. Serve immediately.

Omelette à la crème

Serves 1
Preparation time: 10 minutes
Cooking time: 3-5 minutes

50 g/2 oz cheese, grated

3 tablespoons single cream

3 eggs

3 teaspoons water

salt

freshly ground black pepper

15 g/½ oz butter

4 asparagus spears

1. Mix together the cheese and cream.
2. In a separate bowl beat together the eggs, water, salt and pepper.
3. Melt the butter in an omelette pan and when sizzling hot pour in the egg mixture.
4. Using a wooden spatula keep the liquid egg moving all the time bringing it from the edge of the pan into the centre.
5. When most of the egg has set spread the omelette out to the sides of the pan and allow it to settle for 1-2 seconds, then fold over one-third of the omelette away from the handle.
6. Place half of the cheese mixture along the centre of the omelette and push the omelette down the pan so that it is just coming out of the sides.
7. Hold the pan from underneath the handle and tip the pan over so that the omelette folds out on to a flameproof serving plate.
8. Arrange the asparagus on top and cover with the remaining cheese mixture.
9. Place under a preheated hot grill for a few seconds until the cheese has melted.
10. Serve as a light meal with a salad, or as a main meal with grilled tomatoes and a baked potato.

Granary cheese plait

Preparation time: 30 minutes, plus rising
Cooking time: 35 minutes
Oven: 220°C, 425°F, Gas Mark 7

250 ml/8 fl oz warm water

2 teaspoons sugar

2 teaspoons dried yeast

450 g/1 lb granary flour

2 teaspoons salt

25 g/1 oz lard

1 medium onion, peeled and grated

225 g/8 oz Cheshire cheese, grated

1. Measure the water into a jug. Sprinkle over the sugar and yeast. Leave for about 10 minutes until frothy.

2. Place the flour and salt in a mixing bowl. Add the lard and rub into the flour with the fingertips.

3. Add the onion, cheese and yeast liquid and mix to form a soft dough.

4. Turn out on to a floured surface and knead for about 5 minutes until smooth and elastic.

5. Place the dough in a large oiled polythene bag and leave to rise for about 1 hour until doubled in size.

6. Knead the dough again for 2 minutes and divide into 3 equal pieces. Shape each into a long sausage shape.

7. Plait the pieces of dough together, pinching the ends to seal. Place the plait on a greased baking sheet and cover with oiled polythene. Leave to prove for about 40 minutes until well risen.

8. Sprinkle the plait lightly with flour. Place in a preheated oven and bake for about 35 minutes until golden brown. To test the bread is cooked, tap the base; it will sound hollow when cooked.

9. Cool on a wire tray and serve warm or cold.

Hot cheese & onion bread

Preparation time: 10 minutes
Cooking time: 20 minutes
Oven: 200°C, 400°F, Gas Mark 6

4 spring onions, finely chopped

75 g/3 oz butter, softened

100 g/4 oz Gruyère cheese, grated

salt

freshly ground black pepper

1 small crusty loaf

1. Place the onions, butter, cheese, salt and pepper in a bowl. Beat with a wooden spoon until well mixed.

2. Make cuts down the loaf at 2.5 cm/1 inch intervals almost to the base.

3. Spread the cheese mixture over each slice of bread.

4. Place in a preheated oven and bake for about 20 minutes. Cut into slices and serve immediately.

Leicester scone round

Preparation time: 15 minutes
Cooking time: 25-30 minutes
Oven: 200°C, 400°F, Gas Mark 6

225 g/8 oz self-raising flour

1 teaspoon salt

50 g/2 oz block margarine

175 g/6 oz Leicester cheese, grated

175 g/6 oz cooking apple, peeled, cored and grated

1 egg, beaten

2 tablespoons milk

beaten egg or milk, to glaze

sesame seeds

1. Place the flour and salt in a mixing bowl. Add the margarine, cut into small pieces, and rub into the flour with the fingertips until the mixture resembles fine breadcrumbs.
2. Stir in two-thirds of the cheese and all the apple; mix well.
3. Add the beaten egg and milk and mix to form a soft dough.
4. Turn out on to a floured surface and knead lightly until smooth.
5. Roll out to an oblong, 30 x 23 cm/12 x 9 inches. Sprinkle with the remaining cheese and brush the edges with water.
6. Roll up from one long edge. Place on a greased baking sheet and curl round to form a ring.
7. Make deep cuts around the ring at 2.5 cm/1 inch intervals almost to the base.
8. Brush with beaten egg or milk and sprinkle with sesame seeds. Place in a preheated oven and bake for 25-30 minutes until golden brown. Serve warm.

Peanut cheese biscuits

Makes about 35
Preparation time: 15 minutes
Cooking time: 15 minutes
Oven: 190°C, 375°F, Gas Mark 5

175 g/6 oz plain flour

50 g/2 oz wholemeal flour

½ teaspoon salt

100 g/4 oz butter

1 tablespoon made English mustard

100 g/4 oz Cheddar cheese, grated

75 g/3 oz salted peanuts, finely chopped

1 egg, beaten

2 tablespoons milk

beaten egg, to glaze

1. Place the flours and salt in a mixing bowl. Add the butter, cut into small pieces, and rub into the flour with the fingertips until the mixture resembles fine breadcrumbs.
2. Add the mustard, cheese and nuts; mix well.
3. Add the beaten egg and milk and mix to form a firm dough.
4. Turn out on to a floured surface and knead lightly until smooth.
5. Roll out thinly and cut into 6 cm/2½ inch rounds with a fluted pastry cutter. Gather together the trimmings and cut out more biscuits.
6. Place the biscuits, a little apart, on baking sheets. Brush with beaten egg.
7. Place in a preheated oven and bake for about 15 minutes until golden brown. Cool on a wire tray.

Coffee meringue bombe

Serves 6-8
Preparation time: 20-25 minutes
Cooking time: 45-60 minutes
Oven: 180°C, 350°F, Gas Mark 4

15 g/½ oz butter

25 g/1 oz caster sugar

Meringue:

4 egg whites

50 g/2 oz granulated sugar

1 tablespoon instant coffee
powder

175 g/6 oz caster sugar

Topping:

300 ml/½ pint double or
whipping cream

1 x 300 g/11 oz can mandarin
oranges, well drained, or thin
slices of fresh orange

chocolate dessert topping
(optional)

1. Use the butter to grease a 1 litre/2 pint basin and coat the inside with the caster sugar. Place the basin in a roasting tin with warm water about 5 cm/2 inches up the basin.

2. Whisk the egg whites until stiff.

3. Mix together the granulated sugar and coffee and gradually whisk into the egg whites.

3. Fold in the caster sugar and pour the mixture into the prepared basin.

4. Cook on a low shelf in a preheated oven, for 45-60 minutes, until well risen above the basin and firm to the touch.

5. Remove the basin from the water and leave for 10 minutes, then turn the basin upside down on to a serving plate. Remove the basin when cool.

6. Whip the cream until thick and use to cover the meringue.

7. Decorate with the oranges and dribble the chocolate sauce over.

Almond cheesecake

Preparation time: 30 minutes
Cooking time: 1 hour, plus cooling
Oven: 200°C, 400°F, Gas Mark 6;
160°C, 325°F, Gas Mark 3

100 g/4 oz plain flour

65 g/2½ oz soft (tub) margarine

25 g/1 oz caster sugar

1 egg yolk

Cheesecake:

225 g/8 oz full fat soft (cream) cheese

225 g/8 oz cottage cheese, sieved

100 g/4 oz softened butter

50 g/2 oz ground almonds

few drops of almond essence

4 tablespoons honey

4 eggs, beaten

50 g/2 oz flaked almonds

1. To make the pastry, place the flour, soft margarine, sugar and egg yolk in a mixing bowl. Mix with a fork to form a firm dough.
2. Turn out on to a floured surface and knead lightly until smooth. Form into a round and press evenly into the base of a greased 20 cm/8 inch loose-bottomed cake tin. Prick the pastry with a fork.
3. Place in a preheated oven and bake for 15 minutes until light golden brown. Remove from the oven.
4. Beat together the cheeses and butter until smooth. Stir in the ground almonds, almond essence and honey.
5. Gradually beat in the eggs until the mixture is smooth. Pour into the cake tin and sprinkle evenly with flaked almonds.
6. Reduce the oven temperature and bake for 45 minutes, then turn off the oven and open the door slightly. Cool the cheesecake in the oven.
7. Serve the cheesecake at room temperature.

Coeur à la crème

Preparation time: 10 minutes plus chilling

225 g/8 oz cottage cheese, sieved

150 ml/¼ pint double cream

150 ml/¼ pint soured cream

1 egg white

50 g/2 oz icing sugar, sifted

few drops of vanilla essence

To serve:

caster sugar, optional

double cream, optional

450 g/1 lb soft summer fruits

1. Mix together the cottage cheese, double cream and soured cream.
2. Whisk the egg white until stiff and dry. Whisk in the icing sugar and vanilla essence.
3. Fold the meringue into the cream mixture, cutting through the mixture until all the meringue is incorporated.
4. Have ready 4 heart-shaped coeur à la crème moulds on a tray, or line a large sieve with muslin and place over a bowl. Place the mixture in the moulds or lined sieve, pressing down well.
5. Place in the refrigerator and leave for about 8 hours until the cream is firm.
6. Turn the moulds or mould out on to a serving dish. Sprinkle with a little sugar and pour over a little cream, if liked. Serve with soft summer fruits.

Apricot cream flan

Serves 6
Preparation time: 30 minutes, plus chilling time
Cooking time: 25 minutes
Oven: 200°C, 400°F, Gas Mark 6

200 g/7 oz plain flour
pinch of salt
1 tablespoon icing sugar
100 g/4 oz butter
1 egg yolk
cold water

Filling:

1 egg
1 egg yolk
50 g/2 oz caster sugar
40 g/1½ oz plain flour
300 ml/½ pint milk
2-3 drops vanilla essence

Topping:

1 x 425 g/15 oz can apricot halves, drained, reserving 2 tablespoons juice
5 tablespoons apricot jam
1 tablespoon Cointreau (optional)
25 g/1 oz flaked almonds, toasted
150 ml/¼ pint double or whipping cream, whipped, to serve

1. Sift the flour, salt and icing sugar into a basin. Cut the butter into pieces, add to the flour and rub in, to resemble fine breadcrumbs.
2. Add the egg yolk and enough cold water to mix to a firm dough. Knead well, wrap the dough in foil and chill in the refrigerator for at least 1 hour.
3. To make the filling, put the whole egg, yolk and sugar into a basin and beat until creamy.
4. Blend the flour with a little of the cold milk and stir into the egg and sugar mixture. Bring the remaining milk to the boil and stir into the egg mixture. Return to the saucepan, and stirring constantly, simmer for 2-3 minutes. Stir in the essence.
5. Pour the custard into a basin, cover with a piece of foil or cling film and leave until cold.
6. Roll out the pastry and use to line a 20 cm/8 inch flan ring placed on a baking sheet. Bake blind in a preheated oven for 20-25 minutes. When cooked remove the flan ring and cool the flan case on a wire tray.
7. Transfer the flan case to a plate, fill with the custard and arrange the apricots on top, leaving an edge of custard showing all round.
8. Heat together the apricot jam, juice and Cointreau. Bring to the boil and simmer for 2-3 minutes. When cool spoon over the apricots. Leave to go completely cold.
9. Sprinkle with the almonds. Serve with the cream in a bowl.

Soufflé omelette Grand Marnier

Serves 2
Preparation time: 10-15 minutes
Cooking time: 6-7 minutes

2 eggs, separated

2 teaspoons water

4 teaspoons caster sugar

15 g/½ oz butter

75 g/3 oz fresh fruit, peeled and sliced, or well drained canned fruit, e.g. bananas or apricots

2 tablespoons Grand Marnier, warmed

1. Beat together the egg yolks, water and half of the sugar until creamy and light in colour.

2. Whisk the whites until stiff and fold into the yolk mixture.

3. Melt the butter in an 18-20 cm/7-8 inch omelette pan, pour in the mixture and cook over a low heat until most of the egg mixture has set and the underneath is light golden brown.

4. Put the omelette pan under a preheated hot grill for 1-2 minutes to set the top of the omelette.

5. Make a slit across the centre of the omelette, place the fruit close to the slit and fold the omelette in half away from the pan's handle.

6. Hold the pan from underneath the handle and tilt the pan over so that the omelette falls out on to a flameproof plate.

7. Sprinkle with the remaining sugar, pour over the Grand Marnier and ignite.

Apple & cheese pie

Preparation time: 25 minutes
Cooking time: 35 minutes
Oven: 200°C, 400°F, Gas Mark 6

275 g / 10 oz plain flour

½ teaspoon salt

75 g / 3 oz margarine

50 g / 2 oz lard

3 tablespoons cold water

Filling:

450 g / 1 lb cooking apples, peeled, cored and sliced

½ teaspoon ground cinnamon

100 g / 4 oz soft light brown sugar

175 g / 6 oz Wensleydale cheese, sliced

50 g / 2 oz butter

Glaze:

milk

1. Place the flour and salt in a mixing bowl. Add the margarine and lard, cut into small pieces, and rub into the flour with the fingertips until the mixture resembles fine breadcrumbs. Add the water and mix to form a firm dough.
2. Turn out on to a floured surface and knead lightly until smooth. Wrap in cling film and chill while making the filling.
3. Mix together the apples, cinnamon, brown sugar and cheese.
4. Roll out half the pastry and use to line a 23 cm/9 inch pie plate. Pile half the filling into the pastry case. Cover with cheese slices, then spoon over the remaining filling. Brush the edge of the pastry with milk. Dot the filling with the butter.
5. Roll out the remaining pastry and cover the pie. Press the edges to seal. Trim the edge of the pie with a knife.
6. Gather together the pastry trimmings; roll out thinly and cut into apple shapes. Brush the pie with milk and decorate with the apple shapes, studding each with a clove to resemble a core.
7. Brush the apple shapes with milk to glaze. Sprinkle the pie with sugar. Place in a preheated oven and bake for 35 minutes until the pastry is golden brown. Serve warm with cream.

Sweet cheese with strawberry purée

Serves 6
Preparation time: 10 minutes, plus chilling

225 g / 8 oz ripe strawberries (fresh or frozen), hulled and chopped

50 g / 2 oz caster sugar

juice of ½ orange

450 g / 1 lb medium fat soft (curd) cheese mixed with
6 tablespoons milk or
450 g / 1 lb fromage blanc

mint leaves, to decorate

Fromage blanc can be bought in some large supermarkets and delicatessens. It varies in texture, so if you buy a soft-textured one, serve the dessert in bowls rather than on plates.

1. Press the strawberries through a sieve into a bowl, or liquidize and sieve them.
2. Stir in half the sugar and all the orange juice, then chill.
3. Mix the curd cheese or fromage blanc and remaining sugar together. Divide into 6, shape each into a dome and place on serving plates.
4. Drizzle over the strawberry purée just before serving. Decorate with mint leaves.

Cranberry pancakes

Preparation time: 10 minutes
Cooking time: 15 minutes

100 g/4 oz plain flour

pinch of salt

2 eggs

300 ml/½ pint milk

butter for frying

1 x 375 g/13 oz jar whole
   cranberry sauce

Topping:

150 ml/¼ pint soured cream

2 tablespoons demerara sugar

25 g/1 oz flaked almonds, toasted

½ teaspoon ground cinnamon

2 tablespoons sherry

1. Sift together the flour and salt into a basin. Add the eggs and gradually beat in the milk.

2. In a 13-15 cm/5-6 inch pan, melt a little butter and use the batter to make 8-12 pancakes.

3. Divide the cranberry sauce between the pancakes, roll up and put into a shallow flameproof dish. Keep warm.

4. To make the topping, mix together the soured cream, half of the sugar, almonds, cinnamon and sherry. Pour over the pancakes and sprinkle on the remaining sugar.

5. Put the dish under a preheated grill for several minutes until the sugar has melted and the top is a golden brown.

Notes

1. All recipes serve four unless otherwise stated.
2. All spoon measurements are level.
3. All eggs are sizes 3, 4, 5 (standard) unless otherwise stated.
4. Preparation times given are an average calculated during recipe testing.
5. Metric and imperial measurements have been calculated separately. Use one set of measurements only as they are not exact equivalents.
6. Cooking times may vary slightly depending on the individual oven. Dishes should be placed in the centre of the oven unless otherwise specified.
7. Always preheat the oven or grill to the specified temperature.
8. Spoon measures can be bought in both imperial and metric sizes to give accurate measurement of small quantities.

Acknowledgements

Photography: Robert Golden and Paul Williams
Photographic styling: Antonia Gaunt
Preparation of food for photography: Mary Cadogan and Heather Lambert
The publishers would like to thank the following companies for their help in the preparation of this book: Divertimenti, Marylebone Lane, London W1; Conran Shop, Fulham Road, London SW3; Sloane Square Tiles, Symons Street, Sloane Square, London SW1.

This edition first published in 1986 by
Octopus Books Limited

Published in 1989 by
Treasure Press
Michelin House
81 Fulham Road
London SW3 6RB

ISBN 1 85051 389 9

Printed in Hong Kong